ABANDONED
MAINE

MICHAEL PETIPAS

AMERICA
THROUGH TIME®
ADDING COLOR TO AMERICAN HISTORY

America Through Time is an imprint of Fonthill Media LLC
www.through-time.com
office@through-time.com

Published by Arcadia Publishing by arrangement with Fonthill Media LLC
For all general information, please contact Arcadia Publishing:
Telephone: 843-853-2070
Fax: 843-853-0044
E-mail: sales@arcadiapublishing.com
For customer service and orders:
Toll-Free 1-888-313-2665

www.arcadiapublishing.com

First published 2020

Copyright © Michael Petipas 2020

ISBN 978-1-63499-247-3

Typeset in Trade Gothic 10pt on 15pt
Printed and bound in England

CONTENTS

Dedication **4**

Introduction **5**

1   Battery Steele **7**

2   Big Adventure **17**

3   Deer Camp **29**

4   Evergreen Valley **37**

5   Fort Williams **52**

6   Goddard Mansion **58**

7   Masonry Mill **63**

8   Moulton Sawmill **73**

9   Robinson Mill **80**

10   The Old Farm **88**

About the Author **96**

DEDICATION

This book is dedicated to my wife, Aisling, who has always supported me in all these crazy adventures. None of this would be possible without her.

Painting by Aisling Petipas

INTRODUCTION

The snow had all but melted. The days had become noticeably longer, and the songbirds were breaking the silence of a long, cold winter. It was springtime in New England, and springtime in New England could only mean one thing. It was time for me to get to work shooting my second book, *Abandoned Maine*.

With over 35,000 square miles of land, Maine is the largest of the five states in New England, comprising just under half the area of all the New England states combined. Maine also owns the bragging rights to one of the longest coastlines, not only in New England, but nearly in all the United States, just beating out California with 3,478 miles of coast. Maine is only bested by Florida and Louisiana. Aroostook County in Maine, at 6,453 square miles, is the size of both Rhode Island and Connecticut combined.

As I sat by my woodstove through the long, cold winter, I frequently got on my computer and researched places to visit that would be of interest for the upcoming spring, when I would begin taking pictures again for the new book. I very quickly became aware of the massive size of the state as things I was interested in exploring became spread out from north to south and east to west. I wondered how I would cover so much ground. What had I gotten into? Just to get up into the northern part of the state would take me a whole day of travel either way. Then, of course, there is the always present and very real problem of putting in all this time and effort and coming home empty handed for any number of reasons. This has happened in the past and I was sure it would happen again. I just hoped it didn't happen while I was somewhere south of the Canadian border. The more I thought about it, the more panicked I felt.

In the end, the snow melted and it was time to hit the road. I had my map and somewhat of a plan that would involve working along the coast through the spring and moving inland as summer set in. Finally, I would head up into the north of Maine in the late summer. In the spring, the coast would have less snow than inland Maine and certainly less snow than northern Maine. I would also find accommodations along the coast a lot easier to find in the spring. I have been to various parts of the coast in July and August and it can be extremely crowded; unless you have made reservations weeks in advance, you're probably going to end up sleeping in your car. Inland Maine can get busy through the summer as well, especially around the many lakes that Maine has to offer, but it is nothing compared to the coast. Finally, I would head into the north of Maine to catch the best weather. I figured I would have a better chance of not getting rained out in the latter part of the summer.

Win, lose, or draw, I had to take the bad days with the good days. I had to learn to shrug off the days where I would delete an entire shoot because it wasn't good enough. I needed to learn to put behind me the days where I found nothing I was looking for. Most importantly, I had to learn to embrace the days where I would knock it out of the park, the days that were going to make this book something worth reading.

1

BATTERY STEELE

eaks Island, Maine, is a quaint place located off the coast of Portland. This is the quintessential New England island with a few restaurants to choose from, a coffee shop, and a small grocery store. There are lobster boats moored in Casco Bay and the grey clapboard cottages dot the landscape. People hang brightly colored lobster buoys on white picket fences and driveways are paved with seashells.

The last thing you think of when you first set foot on the island is a massive WWII battery that is hidden away on the back side of the island, overlooking the open water of the Atlantic Ocean. If you take a walk along of the coast, you will come across the occasional forward observation post, but you won't see the battery unless you venture in towards the interior.

Battery Steele today sits neglected and is heavily overgrown with cattail, bittersweet, and wild rose. The 16-inch guns that once protected Portland and Casco Bay have long since been removed. The soldiers that used to outnumber the 700 locals that lived on the island are nothing more than a distant memory for a handful of residents that were around during that time. However, the battery remains an impressive structure with 18-inch steel reinforced concrete walls and a 300-ft. tunnel that runs down the middle of the fortification.

I arrived on the island with my wife, dog, sister, niece, and my sister's husband in tow. I had told my sister, Renee, that her family was welcome to tag along, as long as they remembered that I was out there to do a job.

It was the perfect summer day and we decided to take a walk along the coast and explore the many beaches along the shore of Peaks Island. We skipped rocks, found a rope swing to play on, and looked for creatures in tide pools.

I had managed to get absolutely nothing done and so we decided that lunch at one of the local restaurants on the island was in order. We sat outside on the deck overlooking the harbor and had a wonderful meal, then went for coffee and dessert at the local café.

It was late afternoon by the time I decided to get out to the battery and start working. All day, I kept telling myself that the light wasn't any good and I would wait. This, of course, was just a way to justify my procrastination. When I finally did make it out to what was left of the concrete and steel gun battery, it didn't disappoint.

This was a massive structure and you could still see where the guns would have sat, even though it was heavily overgrown. I put on my headlamp and walked underneath the old battery. The hallway that led from end to end of the old WWII installation seemed to go on forever. The light at the far end of the tunnel looked like nothing more than a pinhole of light.

I began to explore the many rooms that were off to the side of the long hallway. This was some of the best graffiti I had ever seen. There were haunting portraits, large colorful letters, and murals that took up the entire wall of any given room. This went on for the 300 feet of the main hallway and into all the side rooms that were evenly spaced as you walked from one end to the other. As I went from room to room, it became evident that there were a handful of very talented individuals that had been working in these dark and damp rooms under Battery Steele for a long time. The further you explored, the more you would recognize certain individual's works of art by their style. If I were to guess, I would say that there were maybe half a dozen people or less that worked in this space continuously for what must have been years.

I had expected to explore the ruins of an abandoned gun placement when I visited Battery Steele, a military installation that would have the usual amount of spray paint and vandalism you see in all these old concrete dinosaurs of an era gone by. What I didn't expect was that a handful of locals, with names that may never be known, transformed this space into their personal art gallery.

The entrance to Battery Steele where you can clearly see the stamp on the concrete with the date 1942.

Looking down the main hall towards the south end of the battery from the main entrance. If you look closely you can see the exit at the far end of the tunnel.

This is the south battery from the exterior looking in. A massive 12-inch gun would have been mounted on top of this section.

The main entrance looking from the ocean side of the battery. This would have been underneath one of the two guns that used to be mounted here.

Above: One of the many rooms that line the main hallway that runs from end to end of the battery.

Left: This was one of many amazing pieces of art displayed all throughout the fort. Unfortunately, someone decided to deface it.

Standing about halfway down the main hall of the battery. Here you can see a good example of all the rooms that were in this place.

One of the many examples of the painted rooms in Battery Steele.

I really liked this wall. I kept staring at it but couldn't quite figure out why.

These fantastic full wall paintings were represented throughout the whole place.

This was a section of the battery that led to another entrance about halfway between the two batteries. I am not sure what the story is with the table.

There were a series of rooms that were off one of the rooms I was unable to explore because of flooding.

Here is another piece of graffiti art that I really enjoyed.

There were these bits of what looked like wallpaper and posters in some spots throughout the structure. This is also a good example of less talented spray painters.

Looking down the main hallway towards the second gun placement to the south.

This was the south entrance. One of the two main guns would have been mountain above the entrance.

This was the entrance that was located in the middle of the long hallway that ran through Battery Steele. This is where I would have exited if I was able to explore the flooded rooms that are shown in previous pictures.

2

BIG ADVENTURE

Bethel, Maine, is a small mountain town located along the border of New Hampshire and the White Mountain Forest. This picture-perfect New England town is home to many of the things that people love, no matter the season. In the fall, the town and mountains explode into a thousand shades of red, orange, and yellow, making it a key leaf peeping destination. In the winter, Bethel is home to Sunday River, one of the biggest ski resorts in the Northeast. In the summer, you could bring your family to Big Adventure, up until a couple years ago when the amusement park closed for good.

Big Adventure wasn't the biggest amusement park, but it still looked like it would have been a lot of fun. It had everything you could ever want in a park of that size. There were a couple water slides, miniature golf, and a small concession stand. Housed in a rather large red warehouse-style building, there were video games, ski ball, and laser tag. This part of Big Adventure was open year-round.

I pulled into the dirt parking lot of the old amusement park and put my truck in park. I sat there for a minute, marveling at how fast nature had started to claim what was rightfully hers. Big Adventure had only been closed for a couple years, but the amusement park was already heavily overgrown. The miniature golf course was only visible by the breaks in the weeds and briers. The spots where the turf blocked the weeds from growing up looked as if a giant had been walking in circles, pacing back and forth as if waiting for someone who had been late for an appointment.

I shut my truck off and stepped out into the heat of the day. It was around ten in the morning and already the temperature was pushing into the high 80s. It was going to be one of those summer days where you look for water to swim in, shade to sit under, or a room with air conditioning to hide in. I couldn't help but think about how nice it would be if I were here under different circumstances.

I imagined the now boarded-up concessions stand was open. I thought about how I would make my way up to the open window and order a hot dog and an ice-cold Coke. The teenager wearing the paper hat behind the counter would ask if I wanted fries with that. Of course, I would want fries with that. I could almost hear the familiar bells and chimes of games being played nearby. I could hear the fresh clang of quarters as someone put a five-dollar bill into the change machine. I thought about a mom telling her son that this was the last run on the water slide, much to the protest of the young child.

Now the park just sits idle on the side of the road. Small trees have started to grow up around the slides and greenbrier has begun to block the paved walking paths that would lead from hole to hole on the golf course. The pool at the base of the water slides that was once bright blue and crystal clear has been replaced by brackish colored rainwater. There are no more kids splashing into the water as they exit the water slide. There are no more kids laughing as they make their way out of the pool and start sprinting to the top of the slide for another run as the lifeguard yells, "No running!" The only thing there now are the frogs that peer up at you from the grey water that used to be the pool.

Right: Looking at the entrance to the indoor arcade and ticketing.

Below: The side entrance to Big Adventure. The path to the right of the image would lead you around the back side of the building but was most likely used for maintenance.

The pond at the bottom of the two water slides that Big Adventure offered.

Another photo of the swimming pool at the bottom of the two slides, now nothing more than a frog habitat.

Above: The side of the covered bridge that was one of the features of the miniature golf course that ran through the water park.

Right: This is a sign that I have seen many times in many different water parks throughout my life.

Left: The covered bridge appears to have been hole twelve of the miniature golf course. You can still see the sign on the bridge.

Below: The fading turf and holes for the golf balls are still visible in some spots, but it is quickly being reclaimed by nature.

I know that all these yellow flowers are probably just ragweed, but I really liked the way they were taking over.

A sign indicating that you are on the tenth hole of the golf course.

There was a man-made cave that was one of the many great features of this miniature golf course.

This is what is left of the concessions stand. The water slides would have been to the left of the picture.

Looking at the top of the two water slides from the concession stand.

This was a pretty big clue for me as far as what this place used to be called.

Left: Almost to the top. Even though I wasn't going to slide down anything I still got that familiar rush as I almost reached the top of the water slide.

Above: Looking at the underside of the two slides. To the right is a biking path that runs along the river.

Getting ready to head down the water slide.

A picture of one of the turns in the slide near the top. Looks like a lot of fun.

A replica of a water wheel. This was one of the many features on the mini golf course.

Some ragweed pictured in the foreground with the water slides in the background.

Here is another look at the water park from a distance.

3

DEER CAMP

I wasn't happy with the exterior shots that I had taken the day before of Evergreen Valley and had to return to retake the pictures of the outside of the ski lodge. The last thing you ever want to do is re-shoot. The problem was there was terrible lighting and I couldn't quite get the right exposure. The midday sun was creating a brilliant blue sky against the dark brown lodge. My camera could not expose for both, and so I either had a blown-out sky or an underexposed lodge.

I decided that since I had to drive north again in the morning to correct the mistakes of the day before, I would look online and see if there was anything else of interest in the area. I started my usual internet search looking at urbex (urban explorer) pages and then real estate pages in search of abandoned properties that might be close by. Last, I logged onto Google Earth and started scanning around the vicinity of the area. Using Google Earth, I can't see the sides of buildings, but I can see rooftops. A roof that is in disrepair can be the clue that leads you to your next find. I wasn't having much luck finding anything and decided to look at an old logging road I had noticed the day before. I zoomed in and started tracing the dirt road up the side of a small mountain, slowly scanning from where the main paved road ended to where the logging road began. Then, to my surprise, I saw it. About three or four miles up this old logging road in the woods, there was an old rusty roof.

The next morning, I left from the motel early in the morning and headed north with my wife, Aisling, and my dog, Sherman, to investigate what I had seen the night before on Google Earth. I photographed Evergreen Valley for a second time and we headed towards the old skidder road. I pulled off the road and we started uphill into the woods.

We had been walking for over an hour at this point and there was no sign of anything except old stone walls, and where trees had been felled in years past. I didn't have a map or cell service to check my location, so I was going off what I could remember from the previous evening. There was what I would call a main road headed up the mountain and then smaller, overgrown roads that would branch off to the left and right. I started to second guess my direction and was tempted to turn back. I decided that we had come this far, and it was a nice morning for a hike. The dog seemed to be having a great time and maybe there would be a nice view at the top. I didn't want the couple of miles we had already walked into the woods to be a waste.

At this point, we had to be getting close to the top of the mountain and I was sure that the roof I saw must have been on a side trail and we had missed it. I was saddened by the fact that I most likely wasn't going to find answers to this mystery roof when a cabin appeared off to the side of the trail.

I couldn't believe it was up this far. It had an old rusty tin roof and was sided by roofing paper. The walkway up to the front door was overgrown with autumn olive and greenbrier. Parts of the structure were starting to show visible signs of rot. Other than that, this old cabin in the woods seemed to be in decent shape.

I forged my way through the waist-high pickers and walked up to the front door. It was securely fastened with an old padlock. I could see some old bunkbeds through the windows along with a small table in the middle of the room through the dusty and cracked windows.

I refuse to force an entry into a place, even if that means that I have to walk away. The first rule is to never damage anything. I am just there to observe and nothing else. I respect these properties and thus play by the same rules as many other urban explorers.

I noticed one of the windows were open and decided I would go in that way if I had to. This would mean I would have to crawl across the rotten mattresses that were on the bunkbeds and I really didn't want to have to do that.

I decided to take a look around the back side of the old cabin. This was a lot easier going as it sat in the shade most of the day and wasn't really a good growing environment for waist-high plants like raspberry bush and greenbrier.

There was another back door. This was surprising to me that whoever built this place put in two doors on account of how small of a place it was. I walked over and noticed there was no lock on this side. I reached down and turned the doorknob. It rolled over in my hand till I felt the click of the door open. I smiled to myself, knowing that the miles I had just spent walking through the woods were not going to be wasted, and walked into the main living area.

The inside of this old camp was a lot nicer than the exterior would lead you to believe. Whoever had built this place had taken their time. There was an open-hearth fireplace made from granite stone. The main room had knotty pine walls and hard-wood floors with rugs that have since faded in color. The ceiling was made out of Tongue and Groove boards with exposed ceiling joists.

Off to my left was a smaller room about a quarter of the size of the rest of the cabin. This is where the kitchen was located. The same sort of simple but well-done craftsmanship was displayed in here also. There were some cabinets for dishes above an old farmhouse sink. There was a wooden locker-style cabinet for food and on the back wall the cast iron pans hung. On the burner stove sat an old teapot and coffee percolator. I sat there and imagined the low bubbling sound of that old coffee pot as the cabin began to fill up with the smell of the first cup of the day, the hunters slowly rolling out of their bunks and putting on an extra layer of socks to keep their feet warm on those cold November mornings.

I walked back into the living room and that's when I noticed it. On the right side of the mantle of the fireplace sat an obituary of an older man, on a now fading and brown news cutting from the local paper mounted on a flat piece of wood. On the left side of the mantle was a bottle of Redwood Chardonnay with the cork still in it. The bottle of wine was accompanied by a small dusty glass for drinking. The fire was ready to go with wood and kindling in it so that you would just have to hold a match to it.

There was a rocking chair facing the hearth as if waiting for someone.

That old rocking chair was waiting for someone. It was waiting for the man in the faded obituary. It was waiting for him to take a seat to a glass of wine and warm up by the crackling fire after a long day of hunting.

Above: Looking at the old deer camp found in the woods as you approach.

Left: This was the door at the rear of the camp that I found open.

Above: Looking towards the rear of the camp. Judging from the shape of the bunkbeds, I would say no one has been here in quite some time.

Right: Pictured here is the hearth. It had an obituary on the right and a fire that was ready to be lit along with the bottle of wine, glass, and the rocking chair positioned just so.

Looking at the front of the cabin from the doorway leading in. The kitchen was a small separate room from the rest of the cabin.

Pictured here is the kitchen stove and door that would lead into the main part of the cabin right next to the hearth.

Some old pots and pans hanging on the wall of the kitchen that I liked.

There were dishes left in the sink as though someone was supposed to return to this cabin but never made it back.

Looking at the sink and window that would have faced out towards the front of the cabin.

Above left: Notice the old propane light in front of the cabinet. The whole cabin was lit with these old lights.

Above right: There was this old van sitting out back with a bunch of junk in the back of it. I don't really know the story behind this, but I would like to.

4

EVERGREEN VALLEY

Skiing has been popular in New England since the 1920s. Back then, it was a way for people to get together and have some fun. Small outing clubs were formed in towns all over New England and the people would go out and cut a couple trails and maybe put in a rope tow. In the latter half of the 30s, the CCC (Civil Conservation Corp) developed more advanced areas for skiing such as Cannon, Gunstock, and Stowe—ski areas that are still in operation today.

It wasn't until the 1950s and 60s that the ski industry started to really take off. This continued all the way up into the late 80s when there was an absolute bust in the industry with many beloved ski resorts closing their doors for good. As of today, there are roughly 600 ski areas throughout New England that have closed and will never open again. Evergreen Valley was one that didn't make it.

Evergreen was a small ski area boasting only 1,050 vertical feet of drop and accessed by three chairlifts. To put Evergreen's size into perspective, New England's largest ski area, Sugarloaf, boast 2,820 feet of vertical drop and is accessed by thirteen chairlifts. Don't get me wrong—there is nothing wrong with a small ski resort. Many of us here in the northeast have learned to ski at the smaller areas. I myself learned at Gunstock, a smaller mountain located in the lake's region of New Hampshire. The problem with Evergreen, and no doubt contributing to their short run of only ten years of operation from 1972-1982, was not the size of the hill, but rather the opulent base area that accompanied the small mountain. By any standards, this was an extremely ambitious plan for a hill of this size. Evergreen sported a massive base area lodge sporting a price tag of around 7 million dollars for construction that included a year-round heated pool, tennis courts, and later a 9-hole golf course.

Another likely contributing factor was the mountain's location. This is not an easy area to access. You must drive north of Fryeburg, Maine, up towards Keezar Lake.

From there you are on backroads for another half hour as you make your way to the base of Evergreen Valley. You are essentially in an undeveloped part of Maine. There are no restaurants or shops. There is really nothing but old farmhouses occasionally lining the roads. The closest town with amenities would be either Bethel, Maine, to the north, or Fryeburg, Maine, to the south. It would take thirty to forty-five minutes to reach either. I understand there are rural mountains around New England that are self-sustaining, such as Jay Peak in Vermont, but they are three or four times the size of Evergreen Valley. I can only imagine that boredom would set in before lunch for an intermediate to advance skier on such a small mountain. Then what? Take a dip in their heated outdoor pool, get drunk, or maybe take a nap.

All the old ski trails are overgrown today and the three lifts that accessed the mountain were removed in the 90s. However, the base lodge and year-round pool remain, completely untouched. This place is an absolute time capsule. There are no broken windows, no spray paint—none of the usual things you become accustomed to seeing when you visit abandoned places. It becomes evident from the start that the developers of Evergreen Valley spared no expense in the construction of the base lodge. Even by today's standards, it is quite opulent with hanging wagon wheel chandeliers, exquisite woodwork, and a giant open river stone hearth in the bar area. There is abundant natural light that beams through the picture windows that surround the main floor on three sides and allow you to look out at the surrounding mountains.

I imagined that the year was 1982. This was the last year of operation for Evergreen Valley. I see the people dressed in the over-the-top neon ski gear of the day. I imagine people sporting brands like Vuarnet, Oakley, and Revo. They would be grabbing a cup of hot chocolate from the still stacked dishes along the food service area, which would be selling overpriced hot dogs and hockey puck-style burgers that are synonymous with ski lodges all over the Northeast. I could hear the laughter coming from inside the bar, and see the people sitting by the open river stone hearth warming up. I imagined I was there with my friends and we were discussing if we should take another run before the day ended.

I parked over by the old tennis courts of Evergreen Valley. When I walked up for the first time, this was the view of the lodge that I saw. You can see the pool that was heated year-round in the foreground.

The backside of the Evergreen Lodge. The ski trails that are now completely overgrown and no longer visible would have been behind me.

This is the front of the lodge. All these exterior pictures were the second attempt at shooting the lodge. I was unhappy with the exposures on the first day I was up there and so returned to re-shoot the lodge.

Taking a better look at the year-round heated pool. The ski trails would have been located on the hill to the rear of the image. As you can see there is nothing left that resembles a ski trail.

Here is a picture of the cafeteria seating. In the background is the food service counter with the coffee machine and heat lamps visible. This was a familiar scene for me as an avid snowboarder. I could almost taste the overcooked hamburgers and stale coffee.

This was a second room that was adjacent to the cafeteria. The main entrance to the Lodge of Evergreen Valley was to the front of the image.

This is a picture of the ski racks located in the basement of the lodge. I'm not sure if this was a self-serve setup or if there was a ski check here at some point.

The Evergreen Valley logo painted in the basement. I have always loved these ski area logos from the 80s. There is something refreshing about how simple yet effective they all were.

The wagon wheel chandelier. This style of lighting can still be seen in many ski lodges throughout New England. Gunstock, the mountain I grew up riding on, still uses this style chandelier to this day.

Up a set of stairs next to the ticket counter you would find this entrance to the main lodge. The door to the right would lead you to bathrooms and another set of stairs that led to the basement.

This was the second-floor hallway. There were his and her bathrooms to the left as well as another stairway that led to the basement. At the rear, you could exit the lodge to base area.

Here is a picture of a small seating area. The ticket counter is just below this area to the left of the image. To the right is the smaller of the two bars that were in the main lodge area of Evergreen Valley.

Here is another look at that small sitting area that is located just above the ticket counter and main entrance to the ski lodge.

This is a picture of the smaller of the two bars located in the main lodge area of the Evergreen Valley. The small sitting area pictured previously is located behind the stained glass windows.

In the kitchen the dishes were still stacked like they had every intention of re-opening the following fall ski season. Of course, these dishes have been sitting here since the 80s.

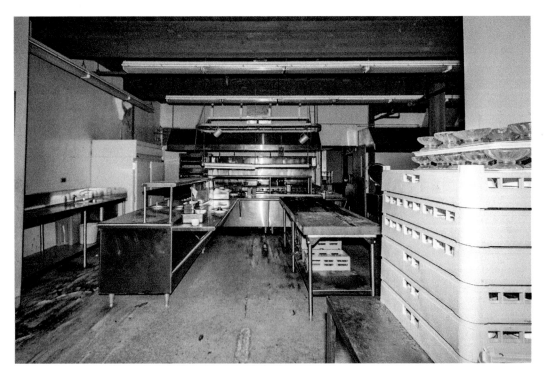

This is another look at the kitchen of Evergreen Valley. Everything is in impeccable condition and it looks like all you would have to do is turn on the lights and gas and start cooking.

It seems like the only thing missing from this kitchen are the pots and pans.

I don't know what this giant pot looking thing is in the kitchen, but it sure looks like it would make a lot of food.

Right: This is the food service counter located in the main lodge area. I remember lining up at many a ski lodge to overpay for what looked and tasted like an overpriced hockey puck style hamburger.

Left: This is the side of the counter that the skiers would be lined up on. I could almost smell the soggy French fries sitting under those heat lamps pictured about mid-image.

This image gives a good perspective of where the food service counter is located within the scheme of the ski lodge. The main kitchen would have been behind the wall behind the counter. The door pictured behind the counter led to the main kitchen.

Above: This is an image of the larger of the two bars that were located in the main lodge area. Behind me was a large open hearth.

Left: This is another look at the larger of the two bars located inside of Evergreen Valley Lodge. Located behind me are large picture windows that looked down on the base of the ski area.

Here you can see the large hearth that was located in the bar. I was able to imagine warming up to a large open fire that crackled and snapped, giving off the soft orange deionizing light of a warm fire.

Another look at the large river stone hearth located in the bar area of Evergreen's main lodge.

This was one of the bathrooms on the main floor of the ski lodge.

Above: This was one of the bathrooms on the main floor of the ski lodge.

Right: This is the ticket counter as you enter the main lodge through a set of large glass doors. The main lodge area provided food service, and seating would have been above you and accessed from a set of stairs off to your left.

5

FORT WILLIAMS

I like to include places in my books that are easily accessible for the readers to check out if they are so inclined. Fort Williams is a must see if you are venturing out and don't want to explore anything too risky. Located on 14 acres in Cape Elizabeth, you can also see Portland Head Light and the Goddard Mansion, located on the same grounds. There is plenty of room for you to run around without being bothered too much by the other people that are there. There are large fields, meticulously maintained gardens, and even a small beach.

It was a beautiful summer day when my wife, Aisling, and I decided to take a drive up to Cape Elizabeth and spend the day exploring Fort Williams Park with our dog, Sherman. We arrived early in the morning in order to beat the crowds. I could tell that it was going to be a wonderful summer day. There was a light breeze coming off the ocean and the fog was just starting to burn off the water. I could see the Goddard Mansion sitting far up on a hill of to my left and what was left of the battery straight ahead as I parked. Portland Head Light House was off to my right. I could only see the top with its light sweeping around.

Fort Williams was in service for the U.S. Army from 1872 to 1964. It was one of many forts and batteries that line the coast of Maine as part of the Harbor Defense Program, designed to protect the Navy ships that were anchored in Portland from 1904-1950. After the fort's closure in 1964, it was purchased by the town of Cape Elizabeth a few years later and converted into the park that it is today.

The original 14 acres of Fort Williams was purchased in 1872 by the U.S. Military as part of the Maine coastal fortifications. It wasn't named Fort Williams until 1899 in honor of the late Major-General Seth Williams of the U.S. Army.

The fort remained relatively unchanged until 1901 when a decade of expansion began to take place. There were many additions to the fort such as: officers' quarters, a hospital, a bakery, a laundry, and a fire station. Then, of course, there was the Goddard Mansion that was at this time housing for non-com officers as well as an officers' club in the basement.

By 1911, Fort Williams had three batteries located in various strategic placements around the now 90-acre military installment. These included Battery Sullivan, Battery Hobart, and Battery Garesche.

During World War I, the fort was fully manned by artillery companies as well as National Guard troops. Anti-aircraft guns were also added at this time. In 1917, two 10-inch guns were removed from Battery Sullivan and two 6-inch guns were removed from Battery Garesche to be send to the Western Front in France to help in the war effort.

Fort Williams again served in WWII as the headquarters for the Harbor Defense of Portland; however, at this time, most of the guns had been removed due to age, becoming obsolete. The more recent batteries such as Battery Steele were to replace the battery at Fort Williams.

The fort remained in service in several different capacities, such as a radar station until 1962, when it was officially closed. The property was sold to the town of Cape Elizabeth a few years later. There was talk of what the town might do with the old military post such as housing, but in the end, it was decided that the grounds would become a park. Most of the buildings that once stood on the grounds have long since been torn down, but the concrete batteries are all still intact. Of course, Portland Light still shines as brightly as the day it was built.

Here I took a long exposure with a neutral density filter. This is looking at one of the batteries that look out to sea.

This steel door was on the opposite bank from the old concrete battery. I'm not sure where it led or what its purpose would have been

Looking at the gun placement as you walk up. I visited Fort Williams early enough in the morning that there were no people around yet. Any later in the day and this picture without people in it would have been impossible.

Another look at the battery from closer. The doorways at the bottom led into small rooms.

Looking at one of the two pillbox emplacements overlooking Portland Harbor. You can see Portland Head Light in the background.

Here I am looking out of one of the pillbox emplacements. There was a commanding view of the surrounding harbor from here.

This was the entrance to the rear of the pillbox emplacements at Fort Williams.

Looking at the gun placement from down by the water. The batteries were placed on higher ground so that when you are in them you are looking down on the ocean.

6

GODDARD MANSION

The Goddard Mansion is an impressive structure that was built for John Goddard from the years 1853-1858. John Goddard a successful lumberman and a colonel that commanded the 1st Maine Volunteer Calvary Regiment for a short time. The Italian-style mansion was built using local stone and is one of the first grand houses on Cape Elizabeth, Maine.

The Army, as part of the nearby Fort Williams, acquired the house in 1898. It was to be used as housing for non-commissioned officers and there was a non-commissioned officers' club in the basement. The house remained property of the United States Army until 1964, when the town of Cape Elizabeth purchased the now decaying mansion, along with Fort Williams.

The old grand house was in derelict shape by the time the town purchased it, although I couldn't seem to find when exactly it was no longer occupied by military personal. I do know that there was a controlled fire lit inside the building in the 80s, most likely to eliminate existing hazards.

It was a beautiful summer day when my wife and I decided to take a drive up to Portland Head Light to check out both the Goddard Mansion as well as Fort Williams. All three of these places are located in the same State-owned park. This is a very accessible spot for anyone to go and visit and I would recommend it if your ever in the Portland area.

Of course, knowing that this place was no secret made me a little skeptical about visiting. I had visited some other military forts and batteries along the coast earlier that week and decided that they were not going to be usable in the book. I feared that I would run into the same issue for the third time that week.

It is easy to explore what is left of Fort Williams without any restrictions; however, in the 90s, they put a security fence around the Goddard Mansion, making it difficult to get inside. I started with some long exposure shots of the fort from a distance and then tried to find my way into the old grand house.

I walked up what used to be the long drive to the house, shooting exterior pictures as I went. I found my wife and dog sitting in the shade of an old willow tree. My wife was painting the old house and my dog was lying in the grass chewing on an old crab leg that he had found on the beach. I stopped to sit with them for a bit and relax.

There was a crowd that had made their way up to the mansion as well and were exploring the outside of the old structure. I decided to wait until the people thinned out to continue taking photos. I don't really want a picture of someone taking a picture.

The people seemed to come and go in these waves of no more than five. I decided that when the group that was up there left, I would have a small window where I could get inside before the next group showed up. I saw the people had finished taking selfies in front of the main entrance to the mansion and were now heading down the hill. I headed around to the back side of the fence that surrounded the place.

On the back side, I found a small enough hole in the fence that I could squeeze through into the interior of the Goddard Mansion. It was overgrown on the inside and the first thing I noticed were the two fireplaces and what remained of the chimneys on the back wall. I am sure this was once two rooms and not one great room. It is highly unlikely that there would be two fireplaces in the same room on the same wall.

I took my time looking around and marveling at the stonework and the perfectly fitted windowsills made from granite. Every stone seemed to fit together like a jigsaw puzzle that had yet to have the image printed on it. Everything was divided by sharp 90-degree angles. It reminded me of one of those M. C. Escher paintings with the optical illusion of there being no beginning and no end to a room. It just seems to go in circles no matter where your eye tracks on the picture.

It's a shame that there were not more efforts to restore this once grand and historic mansion. You can see from the frame of granite stone that this place was a truly exquisite mansion of the day. In the end, it was decided to burn out the interior and leave just the skeleton to sit on the shore of Cape Elizabeth as a monument to days that have passed.

The grounds to the Goddard Mansion were sprawling and well kept. I can only imagine that it is similar if not the same as it was when this was a grand seaside mansion.

This is a picture looking along the front of the mansion. You can see all the intricate stonework that went into the house.

Opposite page, above: There wasn't much left on the inside of the Goddard Mansion. The town of Cape Elizabeth had a controlled fire inside the house in order to mitigate safety hazards.

Above left: I like the angles of this shot looking from the exterior into the main part of the house. It also shows the attention to detail that the stone masons paid to the work they were doing.

Above right: I took this picture because I really liked the brickwork running down the center of the widows throughout the Goddard Mansion.

Above: Here is another look at the stonework around the windows. All the windows were dressed in this way.

Left: Looking from the far end of Goddard Mansion. It appeared from the remains of this grand old house, there were many rooms in the interior. Sadly, I was unable to find any images of what the house originally looked like on the inside.

7

MASONRY MILL

Every now and then, while I'm looking for abandoned places, I will get lucky and stumble across something that I didn't know I was looking for. This was the case with the old stone mill that I happened upon while up in Bethel, Maine. I had originally gone up that way to visit the abandoned remains of Big Adventure amusement park.

I had finished shooting Big Adventure for the day and my wife and I were looking for a place to grab lunch. We drove from the amusement park back into the center of town with no real plan as to where we were going to stop. We passed by a small coffee shop and decided that an iced coffee would be perfect on this unusually hot day.

I pulled my truck into a parking spot on Maine St. and waited while my wife ran in to ask if the dog could join us in the outside seating area. I pulled out my phone and did a quick search of the area on Google Earth to see if I could find something else to explore.

I scanned up and down the roads that were just outside of town looking at all the rooftops. I wasn't finding much until I moved my cursor over to the Androscoggin River that runs through Bethel, Maine. I started to follow the river west into the interior of Maine.

I stopped on a large complex of some sort that had two or three silos and close to a dozen outbuildings sitting on maybe 10 or 15 acres. The rooftops looked like they were in decent shape; however, the grass had not been mowed in quite some time and there were no cars in the parking lot. This looked like a spot worth checking out.

We finished our lunch and I told my wife there was one more spot that I wanted to investigate before we headed south for the day. She agreed, even though I knew all she really wanted to do was spend the afternoon soaking in a swimming hole in one of the many rivers that dot this part of the state. I can't say that I blame her—that was all I wanted to do as well, but as we were a few places short of a book we went for it.

The first building that greeted me as I ducked under the main gate was what I am guessing was the main office. Beyond that, I could see an open room where you could walk in one side and walk out the other looking at all the types of stone that this place offered. The various samples were still lined up on the shelf, all neatly packaged with bright green labels on the top of the display boards giving a brief description as to what kind of stone it was and what might be some of its uses.

From there, I started to just wander around, going from building to building. Most were open and you could just walk right in. I found where there were stacks of pallets stored for shipping. I discovered an old boiler sitting there with the doors wide open. I found a back office with a chair made from skis tucked into the back of what might have been a maintenance shop. In one of the last buildings I looked in, there was a green Porsche, covered in dust and just below a large yellow sign that read: "SAFTEY." I couldn't believe what I was looking at. Why would you just leave a car like this?

I wandered around for a bit longer, taking some pictures and wondering why this place had closed. It looked like it must have been a large and profitable business not too long ago. Perhaps the operation just moved to a different location. I looked online, but could only find an old website from when the place was open, and a real estate ad for the sale of the property.

This is an image of a garage building that sat towards the far end of the sprawling Masonry Mill complex.

Towards the front of the image in the open bay doors there are a bunch of crates filled with granite boulders. They were all lined up as if a truck was going to pick them up that afternoon.

This picture was taken on the backside of the complex. This image gives a good vantage of the two silos.

I loved the industrial look of the whole complex. As I wondered around the large complex, I marveled at all the machinery and conveyors that were used in this operation.

Inside one of the buildings towards the main entrance to the plant, I found this old boiler. I'm guessing that it was used to power the equipment in the operation.

Here is another image of the boiler I found in one of the many rooms I explored.

Above left: This is an image of the backside of the boiler. The main steam lines that come off the back of the boiler would leave the building that the boiler was in and travel all over the complex.

Above right: I loved the angle of the pipes coming off the rear end of the boiler mixed with the fading steel.

Here is an image looking at the room from the rear of the room that the boiler sat in. In the foreground is most likely a water tank that fed the boiler to make steam.

This was a large sprawling space I found. I am guessing it was warehouse storage of some type.

Looks like someone forgot were they parked their Porsche. I couldn't believe what I was looking at when I found this.

Clearly this was where the wooden pallets were stored.

This image gives a good perspective as to how large this place was.

Above: Looking back at the garage with the name of the operation on it. The garage at the far end of the image is where I entered the property.

Left: These are large masonry saws. The blades that would have sliced through brick or cinderblock have been removed. These work in the same way a miter saw works where you lower the large circular blade down onto the table to make the cut.

This was an open-ended showroom showing off the many products that Masonry Mill offered when it was in operation.

I found this back office in what looked like it must have been a maintenance building of some sort.

The logo of the Masonry Mill Corp. This was on the back of a garage that sat away from the rest of the complex.

8

MOULTON SAWMILL

Maine is known for its timber industry in the northeast, dating back as far as the seventeenth century when settlers first started cutting trees on Monhegan Island. The first official sawmill in Maine was built in 1634. By 1830, Bangor, Maine, was the world's largest lumber shipping port. The Moulton Sawmill was one of the many mills that were in operation in the state during this era.

Built in 1790, Moulton Sawmill was originally known as Adams Sawmill. Later, in 1882, it became Moulton Sawmill. The mill operated until the 1980s, when the state shut the operation down due to pollution from sawdust entering the waterway that powered the mill.

I found out about the old sawmill from the caretaker of the old Robinson Mill that I had visited a week or so before, but I wasn't going to have time to drive down to Parsonfield that afternoon and visit the mill, because it was getting late. I decided I would return to that part of Maine a couple weeks later on my way over to Kennebunk.

I left for Maine a couple weeks later, as I had planned. I headed east towards Tamworth, New Hampshire, where I would drive across Route 25 and into Porter, Maine. From there I would drop south a bit and check out the old sawmill. As far as looking for places, this one wasn't hard to find. I basically would have driven by it whether I was looking for it or not.

This abandoned sawmill did not disappoint. The trees were just coming into bloom and the mill reflected off the pond that sat at the front of the decaying structure nicely. I was happy with the pictures I was getting of the exterior from the front.

I was making my way around the side of the building and had yet to find a way in. This was starting to make me nervous. I would have these great exterior shots that I couldn't use. If I couldn't get into the building it was unlikely that I would be able to use it for the book.

I made my way to the back of the Moulton Sawmill where the old mill sits elevated off the water on big 12 x 12 beams. There was an opening I could get through, but it was 10 or 15 feet off the ground. At this point, I had two choices. I could scrap the whole thing, or I could try and scale the side of the half-rotten mill.

I put my camera into the backpack I was wearing so that it wouldn't get banged up in my attempt. I was going to have to take a running start and use the old granite block that was used as a footing for the post as a kind of springboard. I hoped that I would have enough vertical reach to grab onto the windowsill above me. I took a step back and sprung forward. My foot hit that granite post and I leaped up with all I had. I grabbed the windowsill above me and just hung there. I had not really come up with a start-to-finish plan on this one. I figured that if I got started, the rest would work itself out. It had not, and I was just hanging off the side of the building, not knowing what to do next. My camera bag was too heavy. It was dragging me back off the wall I was hanging from. My grip let go and I fell backwards into the mud and water below me.

I needed a new plan: I took my camera backpack off and hung the camera around my back and then secured it by wrapping the mud-soaked jacket around the camera and then my waist. Next, I looked around for something that might help boost me up through the window. I found an old rusty framing nail among the rubble that was outside the building and hammered it into a beam with a rock as high up as I could reach.

I took a step back and lunged forward, launching myself upwards towards the windowsill once again. I searched around with my foot for the nail and lifted myself up to where I had enough room to pull myself the rest of the way through the window. I dropped on my side into a pile of old sawdust that was covering the floor and lay there for a minute, catching my breath. I wished that someone was there to give me a high five on my feats of strength, but it was just me laying in the sawdust and dirt, covered in mud and wondering how the hell I was going to get out of here again.

I had landed in the part of the mill where they would stack lumber after it had been cut, most likely to cure. There were still boards stacked up and large double bay doors that led to the exterior of the mill. I began taking pictures while making my way to the large open door that led to the main part of the sawmill. The building had split apart here and there was a three or four-foot gap separating the two rooms. I knew if I wanted to get into the rest of the mill I was going to have to jump across the gap. Usually you slowly make your way across these old wooden floors as if they were thin ice. Jumping can be the most dangerous thing to do. I really have no way to know what condition the floor is in.

I inched my way up to the gap in the floor and immediately felt this wave of anger come over me. It was clear that this old sawmill wasn't going to make it easy for me. Most of the sawmill was on the other side of this gaping hole in the floor. If this place was going to make the new book, I had to get to the other side of that open door. Sometimes, it's best to not think too long on a bad decision. I stepped back a couple paces to get a running start and leapt into the next room.

I was now standing in the main part of the Moulton Sawmill. The first thing I noticed was what I assume is an old belt driven planer. The space was dimly lit with rays of sunshine breaking through the dusty old single-pane windows. There was a peaceful light in this space.

I stayed inside the old sawmill for a long time, shooting everything at least three times. I didn't want to miss anything, and I certainly didn't want to have to repeat getting into this space. Better safe than sorry.

I made my way out the same way I had come into the Moulton Mill and returned to where I had parked. My wife, Aisling, was sitting on the tailgate of my truck painting an old barn that was next to the mill. My dog was sleeping under the tailgate in the shade. He got up wagging his tail when he saw me approach. I was wet and covered in mud from my first attempt at getting into the Moulton Sawmill, but it was worth it. I had gotten the pictures I came there for and was grateful that I came out in one piece.

Moulton Sawmill has one of the coolest exteriors I have seen. It almost looks like a building out of a child's imagination.

The sawmill was powered by the waterway pictured here.

Pictured here is the main entrance to the sawmill. Behind the building to the right is where I climbed up and through the window.

I found this old work bench sitting in the main part of the mill. Scattered on the floor appear to be old leather drive belts.

Above left: Found this old 5-gallon oil can sitting on a bench.

Above right: This is one of the saw blades that would have been used to mill the trees.

Pictured here is an old belt driven lathe that is used to smooth boards once they are cut to the proper dimension.

This is a picture of various bits and pieces that I found lying on the floor.

Looking at the back side of the mill you can see that it is quite a bit larger than it appears from the front of the building.

9

ROBINSON MILL

I have driven by the Robinson Mill in Parsonsfield, Maine, for years. Every time I go to Maine, it seems like I always take the same route. I usually cross the NH/ME boarder around Effingham, New Hampshire, and head west towards the coast. In going this way, I have driven by this old textile mill many times, but never bothered to stop.

On a trip back from the Camden area of the state I decided that I would check it out on my way back through. It had been a pretty good week shooting north of Portland along the coast. It was one of those trips where all my initial leads turned out to be a waste of time, but then you find other abandoned buildings that made the whole trip. On this trip was when I discovered the old farmhouse that's also in the book while looking for something else.

It was just after noon when I pulled into the lower parking lot of the old textile mill. It was a wonderful spring day and the sound of the water from the river that once powered the mill broke the silence of the day with the white noise of a feverish spring runoff. I noticed there were large old electric motors lined up against an old retaining wall as if they were rusting soldiers waiting for orders.

I noticed that these old electric motors still had visible manufacturing stamps that said Davis and Furber. Davis and Furber Manufacturing was a massive industrial complex in Andover, Massachusetts, built in 1828, and remained in operation until the 1980s. They were known for making equipment that would keep the many textile mills throughout New England in operation. However, with the death of the textile industry in New England to foreign markets came the death of the companies that worked in support of these mills.

I had not been there long when a women came out of the interior of the mill complex and approached me exclaiming that I was on private property. I had seen the giant NO TRESSPASSING sign spray painted on the side of the mill when I drove in, but I would choose to leave that out of the conversation we were about to have.

As it would turn out, the women who looked like she was going to give me the boot at first was, in the end, very accommodating. She was a photographer herself and when I told her the reason that I was there, she introduced herself and told me her name was Megan. She agreed to show me around the old textile mill that her family had purchased in order to repurpose it. Megan had been hired on by her family as the caretaker for the massive facility. She told me that her family had plans of turning the old textile mill into housing and some other facilities.

We began to walk around the sprawling complex, talking about things both related to the mill and things we had in common. Megan enjoyed taking pictures throughout the seasons of the mill and had some really great shots from the fall during peak foliage. I was a little jealous that I wasn't going to be able to get those peak foliage images shot through the giant mill windows.

There are some old looms and motors lying about and parts of an old elevator inside the massive building, but other than that it is mostly cleared out. You must use your imagination as to what floor after floor of vast empty space was like when this place was in operation.

The Robinson Mill wasn't actually the Robinson Mill until 1972 when it was purchased by the Robinson family. From 1880 until then, it was known as Kezar Woolen Manufacturing.

The Robinson Manufacturing Company was one of the oldest family-run companies in Maine. They operated a similar mill in Oxford, Maine, from 1863 up until that mill closed its doors in 2003. The mill in Oxford was one of the last textile mills to close down in New England. It is said that the Robinson Manufacturing Company produced the beautiful oxford blue woolen twill that did not fade for the Union Troops during the Civil War.

The more of these mills I visit and the more I learn about them, the more I start to realize how important they are to New England's history. It feels like people have already started to forget about these old textile mills.

As recently as the early and mid-90s, a lot of these mills were still in operation. These textile mills in some cases would employ a major percentage of the population that live in the smaller mill towns throughout New England. In a lot of cases these textile mills were partly responsible for shaping these tiny river towns into what they are today.

The textile mills in New England have seen the last of the shift whistle blow in my lifetime. There are many people that still live in small towns like Parsonfield, and many other towns like it, that once worked in these factories. There are people that drive by their former place of employment every day and watch their memories turn to dirt. They watch as roofs cave in, windows break, and exteriors get spray-painted by vandals with nothing better to do.

Pictured here are one of about a half-dozen carding machines that were still on the premises. Carding machines were used to detangle, clean, and intermix the fiber in a textile operation.

An exterior picture of the front of the Robinson Mill.

This was an old office chair that was just sitting in the middle of the bottom floor of the old textile mill. I found it somewhat awkward that it was just sitting in the middle of this large vacant space.

Above left: There were these two colorful doors just sitting up against a wall with no door openings anywhere near where they were found.

Above right: This is a picture of one of what I assume to be one of the boiler doors. This was just sitting on the floor and I never found the boiler.

Above: Pictured here is the first floor of the old textile mill.

Left: I found these two bathrooms on the third floor. I assume that blue is for men and pink is for the ladies.

The lettering on the floor of the third floor of the Robinson Mill is a mystery. I asked around, but no one seemed to know what this would have been used for.

Looking out massive windows on the main level that line each floor of the textile mill.

This place used to be a massive operation with four floors of production, not including the basement. Pictured here is the second floor.

Here is another picture of one of the large carding machines.

Another picture of the front of one of the carding machines. The old wool bits are still stuck to the spool.

Right: The manufacturing tag clearly reads Davison and Furber on this carding machine. This was a textile company out of Andover, Massachusetts, that made a lot of textile machinery from 1832-1908.

Below: Here is a wide-angle picture of the Robinson Mill.

10

THE OLD FARM

Just north of Camden, Maine, on Route 1, there is an old farmhouse sitting on the side of the road. The front porch has caved in and the paint has been peeling away for quite some time. There are some old apple trees behind the house and the yard has been overgrown with weeds and greenbrier. I surmised no one had lived here for quite some time, but it still felt as though I was being watched from the minute I set foot on the property.

The curtains were drawn on the windows, but I continued to scan for a hand that would pull one back just enough to peak out at whoever was in the front yard, although I was certain that there was no one in there. The hair on the back of my neck stood up and I quietly hoped that I wouldn't be able to get into this place.

Camera in hand, I walked up to the front door where the porch had collapsed. I tried the door, but it was locked. I shot some exterior pictures and made my way to the rear of the house through waist-high greenbrier that raked at my arms and legs as I forged through it. On the back side of the house, the breezeway that separated the house from the barn had collapsed, leaving a gaping hole into the interior of the house. This was a way in.

There was quite a bit of rubble in the way of the entrance to the main house. I climbed over the broken timbers and remnants of the collapsed roof on the ground, and pushed my way through the door that led into the interior of the old farmhouse.

I found myself standing in what looked like an old utility room. I could see an old fridge sitting in the adjacent room, one of those antique fridges with the big stainless-steel handles on the front that they had to discontinue selling, because kids would get locked inside them playing hide and seek and suffocate. The feeling that I was not alone in this abandoned farmhouse was making it difficult for me to move forward. Every part of me wanted nothing more than to turn back. I wanted nothing to do with this place. I don't know what happened here, but it was not inviting in any way.

I was sweating and my mouth was dry. I tried to say out loud to myself that there was no such thing as ghosts to reassure myself, but I was too scared to speak. I didn't want to make a sound. I didn't even want to walk forward for fear of creaking floorboards. Maybe, I thought to myself, if I'm really quiet, the spirits won't know I'm here.

I was shooting fast with my Nikon, using autofocus and only a single flash, and I had the camera shutter set to high speed. I was just holding down the shutter release and canvasing the room like I was shooting a machine gun at an invisible enemy. The only sound in the room was the click of the ten frames a second.

There were all sorts of papers strewn all over the floor like a strong wind had blown through the house; however, this couldn't have been the case as all the windows were intact and all were closed. There was an old chair sitting next to the window positioned so that you would be able to look out the window towards the street. I imagined a lonely old woman just sitting there for hours watching life pass by outside her living room.

From the living room, I followed the piles of strewn newspapers, pamphlets, and torn-out pages of books into the kitchen. There was an empty cabinet sitting on the back wall and there were old Ball jars with preserved vegetables still in them. It seemed like the further into this house I ventured, the worst my anxiety got. I really didn't like those preserves left behind. What happened? Why would you leave your food for winter behind? My imagination was getting the best of me and these were not pleasant thoughts.

I then entered the last room on the far side of the farmhouse and found an old standup radio—the kind that the whole family would sit around in the 50s and tune in to their favorite program. There was a piano and another chair sitting next to that old radio, as though someone had been listening to it recently. I held my camera to my eye and repeated the same sort of machine gun attack on this room. I wanted to get the hell out of there as soon as possible. I would sort out the hundreds of images later in the safety of anywhere but here.

Without knowing the story behind this old farmhouse. I can only use my imagination and clues left behind to make up my own story. What I do know is this place was creepy. Even as I sit here writing this, I feel anxious thinking back to that day in early spring along the coast of Maine.

Above: A picture of the front side of the old farmhouse that I discovered just outside of Camden, Maine.

Left: Looking at the fridge in the kitchen. If the age of this kitchen appliance is any indicator of how long this place has been abandoned, then it has been unoccupied for quite some time.

This is a picture of what was left of the living room. There where pages from the newspaper and magazines scattered all over the room like a stiff breeze had blown through.

This old piano was found in at the farthest room back in the farmhouse. The door to the rear of the room leads to a bathroom.

Above left: Another picture of the piano found in the back room of this house. You can partly see into the only bathroom on the first floor.

Above right: A black-and-white image of the piano found in the back room.

Above left: This is a wide-angle shot of what I assume is the old living room. Through the door next to the second fridge is the utility room or what is often referred to in New England as the mudroom.

Above right: I didn't spend much time on the second floor due to the advanced stages of rot in the house. I didn't feel like falling through the ceiling to the floor below on this particular day. This was one of the bedrooms I found upstairs.

Above: The canned food was still lined on the shelves and scattered on the floor as if whoever left had planned on returning after a short while. If you look closely, the paper on the floor has the year 1991.

Right: This is a picture of the pantry that was located just behind the kitchen.

Another picture of the upstairs bedroom. The split lath and plaster in the ceiling gives a clue as to how old this house is. This was a popular building technique used around the turn of the century up until around the 1930s.

Above: This little window looked into one of the two bedrooms that were on the second floor of the old farmhouse. This picture was taken from the top of the stairs.

Left: A photograph of the old fridge found in the kitchen.

Opposite page, below:

Left: A black-and-white image looking at an old apple tree and the side of the house that I walked around to gain access though the collapsed breezeway.

Right: Here is another shot of the old apple tree and farmhouse from the side.

This is a picture of the back wall of the mudroom. This room separated the old barn and house via a small breezeway. This is also very common in houses that were built at the turn of the century

ABOUT THE AUTHOR

MICHAEL PETIPAS was born in Boston, Massachusetts. At the age of four, his family moved to rural New Hampshire, where he grew up on a 60-acre farm. His life on the farm shaped his love of nature and his creative spirit. Michael's love of photography was encouraged by his beloved grandfather, Vincent Petipas, who worked as a professional photographer in Boston. Michael continues to find inspiration in the natural beauty of New England and spends many hours hiking in search of the perfect shot. Michael lives in the Lakes Region of New Hampshire, with his wife, Aisling (also an accomplished artist), his dog, Sherman, and his cat, Mayonnaise.